HOW TO LOOK AFTER YOUR PET

GUINEA PIGS

GUINEA PIGS

Mark Evans

B.Vet.Med.

DORLING KINDERSLEY

**LONDON, NEW YORK, MUNICH, PARIS,
MELBOURNE AND DELHI**

A DORLING KINDERSLEY BOOK
www.dk.com

For my brother, Andrew

Project Editor Liza Bruml
Art Editor Jane Coney
Editor Miriam Farbey
Designer Rebecca Johns
Photographer Paul Bricknell
Illustrator Malcolm McGregor

Published in Great Britain by
Dorling Kindersley Limited
A Penguin Company
80 Strand, London, WC2R 0RL

8 10 9 7

Colour reproduction by Colourscan, Singapore
Printed and bound in Spain by Artes Gráficas Toledo, S.A.
D.L. TO: 149-2002

Models: Narada Bernard, Jacob Brubert, Jade Carrington,
Martin Cooles, Laura Douglas, Angelina Halkou, Louisa Hall,
Thanh Huynh, Gupreet Janday, Rachel Mamauag,
Paul Mitchell, Serena Palmer, Florence Prowen,
Isabel Prowen, Jamie Sallon, Lisa Wardropper

Dorling Kindersley would like to thank Peter Gurney
for supplying guinea pigs, Wood Green Animal Shelters,
The Cambridge Cavy Trust, Christopher Howson for design
help, Bridget Hopkinson for editorial help, Salvo Tomasselli
for the world map and Lynn Bresler for the index.

Picture credits: Walter Büchi p12 tl, tr; Steve Shott p25 c

Note to parents

This book teaches your child how to be
a caring and responsible pet owner. But
remember, your child must have your
help and guidance in every aspect of day-
to-day pet care. Don't let your child keep
guinea pigs unless you are sure that your
family has the time and resources to look
after them properly – for the whole of
their lives.

Contents

Introduction

The first step to becoming a good guinea pig owner is to choose the right kind and number of pets. Guinea pigs with short hair are the easiest to care for. A guinea pig likes to have company, so you should get at least two. But remember, whatever kinds and however many pets you choose, you'll need to look after them every day. Not just to start with, but for the whole of their lives.

Shopping basket full of things you will need

Understanding your pets

You have to get to know your guinea pigs. If you handle them gently and talk to them as much as you can, they will quickly learn to trust you. Watch them very carefully, and you will soon begin to understand the many fascinating ways that they talk to each other.

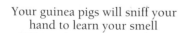

Your guinea pigs will sniff your hand to learn your smell

Caring for your pets

You will only be your pets' best friend if you care for them properly. You will need to make sure that they eat the right foods, always have water, and get plenty of exercise every day. You will also have to groom them regularly, and keep their hutch clean.

You will have to groom your guinea pigs every day

Things to do with your pets
Your guinea pigs are very active. You should play with them in their fun box and enclosure every day. If you keep them busy, you will show everyone that you are a good pet owner.

Hiding food is a favourite game

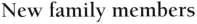

People to help
The best guinea pig owner always tries to find out more about her pets. You can ask your vet and nurse how to keep your guinea pigs healthy and happy.

You will need to visit your vet centre regularly

New family members
Your guinea pigs will be a very special part of your whole family. Everyone will want to stroke them, and be interested in what they do. They can even become good friends with some of your other pets.

Ask a grown-up
When you see this sign, you should ask an adult to help you.

Your pets will become part of your family

Things to remember
When you keep guinea pigs, there are some important rules you must always follow:

❀ Wash your hands after stroking or playing with your pets, and after cleaning their hutch.

❀ Don't kiss your guinea pigs.

❀ Never give your guinea pigs food from your plate.

❀ If your guinea pigs are hiding or in their beds, don't annoy them.

❀ Never tease your guinea pigs.

❀ Always watch your guinea pigs when they are with other pets.

❀ Never, ever hit your guinea pigs.

What is a guinea pig?

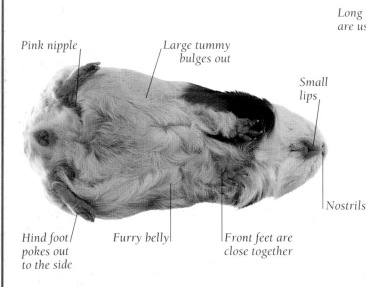

The guinea pig is not really a pig at all. It is a rodent and its proper name is a cavy. Rodents have very sharp front teeth that never stop growing. They are used for gnawing. All rodents belong to a group of animals called mammals. Mammals have warm blood and a hairy body. When young, they drink milk from their mothers.

Small and tubby

A guinea pig has a plump body. It has short legs, so it is not good at running a long way or climbing. A guinea pig's neck is very short and its mouth is very near the ground, so that it doesn't have to bend down to graze on grass.

Long eyebrows are used to feel

Pink nipple

Large tummy bulges out

Small lips

Nostrils

Hind foot pokes out to the side

Furry belly

Front feet are close together

Long whiskers bristle out to feel

Sharp claws give a good grip on rough ground

Underneath your guinea pig

A guinea pig has a great, big stomach where tough plant food is digested. It is so large that the back legs have to point sideways to fit round it. The front feet are close together. They lift the head off the ground. Look closely at the tummy and you should see two nipples. In a mother guinea pig, they are sucked for milk by her babies.

Ear hears the
faintest sounds

Always alert
A guinea pig can detect
danger, even when eating
with its head down. It
has good hearing and a
very keen sense of smell.
Its eyes are on the sides
of its head, so it can tell
if something creeps up
from behind.

Eye keeps
watch for
enemies

Nose sniffs
the weakest
of smells

Whiskers sense
danger around face

Large mouth
has room for
20 teeth

Thick, furry coat helps keep
the guinea pig warm

Grease gland makes
a smelly wax

Eyelids clean
dust from the
eye when the
guinea pig blinks

The front teeth
keep growing.
Gnawing grinds
them down

The big back foot
has three toes and
a leathery sole

The front foot
has four toes.
Leathery pads
protect the fine
toe bones

Large tummy
hides back legs

A guinea pig's
tail is so short
you can't see it

When a guinea
pig stands up,
you can see its
long back legs

11

Life in the wild

Wild guinea pigs live in family groups in the high mountains and the flat grasslands of South America. A long time ago, they were bred for food by the local people. Traders took wild guinea pigs from South America all over the world. The guinea pigs that we keep today as pets are descended from these wild guinea pigs.

Natural home

Wild guinea pigs trample down the grass around their homes to make paths, called runways. They live in the tall grass, or in the old burrows of other animals.

Wild ancestor

The wild guinea pig is smaller and has a more pointed snout than the pet guinea pig. Its coarse fur may be brown, black or grey. Each hair has a light tip, which makes the coat look speckled.

Tall, dry grass is easy to flatten

Guinea pig looks out curiously

Guinea pig sits in hollowed-out grass runway

Guinea pig likes to hide away

Hiding away

Guinea pigs are very timid. They spend a lot of time hiding in grass. They sleep for about five hours a day, but they never close their eyes for more than ten minutes!

Guinea pig's favourite pastime is nibbling

Nibbling morning and evening

Guinea pigs eat for about six hours every day. They feed in dim light, mainly at dawn and dusk, when their enemies find it difficult to see them.

Friendly group

When they are not eating or sleeping, guinea pigs like to be with their families and friends. They huddle together, play, and go exploring.

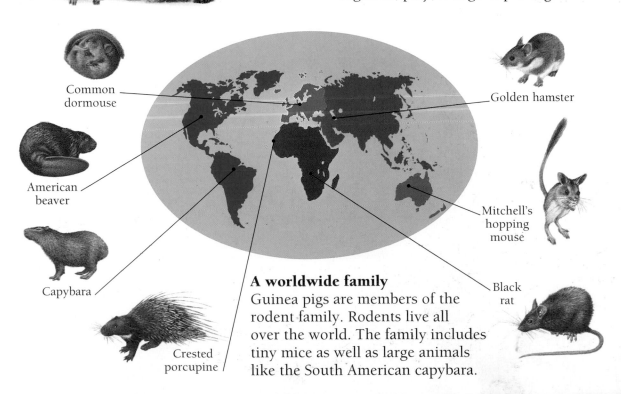

Common dormouse

Golden hamster

American beaver

Capybara

Mitchell's hopping mouse

Black rat

Crested porcupine

A worldwide family

Guinea pigs are members of the rodent family. Rodents live all over the world. The family includes tiny mice as well as large animals like the South American capybara.

All colours and patterns

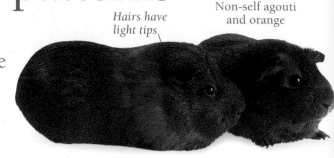

Hairs have light tips

Non-self agouti and orange

There are many kinds, or breeds, of guinea pig. Some have a single-coloured coat. These are called "self" types. "Non-self" types have up to three colours in their coats. Guinea pigs also have different hair styles – short, long, tufty and wiry. Think carefully before choosing guinea pigs with long hair. Their shaggy coats need a lot of extra care.

Agouti guinea pigs
The hair on agoutis changes in colour from the root to the tip. This makes them look speckled. All wild guinea pigs are agoutis.

Shiny coat is orange

Black bottom

Black patch

Brown patch

White band around middle

Short-haired guinea pigs
Short-haired guinea pigs have a smooth, glossy coat. The coat patterns have names, such as Dutch and tortoiseshell.

White patch

Non-self Dutch

Self golden

White stripe

Non-self Tortoiseshell and white

Ridge along spine

Fur stands on end

Smart brown tuft on head

Self white Abyssinian

Non-self tortoiseshell and white Abyssinian

Abyssinian guinea pigs
All the hair on your head grows from one centre that is called a hair crown. Abyssinian, or rough-coated guinea pigs, have many hair crowns all over their bodies. This makes their coats look very tufty.

Coat is made up of swirls of black and orange hair

Non-self tortoiseshell Abyssinian

14

Crowning crests

Some guinea pigs have a special hair crown on the top of their heads. This is called a crest.

Golden crest

Non-self crested Dalmatian

Self crested ruby

Two guinea pigs of the same breed produce an identical pig

The pig looks the same as its parents

Long, soft hair

Non-self Peruvians

Peruvians

Peruvian guinea pigs have silky hair that grows down to the ground. The fringe must be brushed back to stop it covering their eyes.

Grey and white hair is short on face

Non-self Sheltie

Two different breeds of guinea pig produce a mix, or crossbred

The pig looks a little like both of its parents

Shaggy Shelties

Shelties have very long coats, but their hair does not grow over their faces. They can see where they are going more easily than Peruvians.

White coat with brown spots

Silky fur feels smooth

Silky satins

Some guinea pigs have very soft and shiny fur. These are called satins.

Non-self Dalmatian satin

Self ruby satin

Non-self agouti rex

Two crossbred pigs can have almost anything

A real mixture!

Wavy rexes

Rex guinea pigs have short, thick hair. Their wavy coats feel coarse when you stroke them.

Self ruby rex

Non-self Dutch rex

Your guinea pigs' home

Before you collect your guinea pigs, you must get them a hutch to live in. They are very active, so the hutch must have plenty of space. Put the hutch in a sheltered place, where it is safe from other animals. Remember to stock up with guinea pig food (see p26). You also need to buy bedding and feeding equipment.

Roof slopes so that rain runs off

Solid door helps keep room warm

Bedroom for sleeping and hiding away

Check the size of the hutch before you buy

A branch from a fruit tree, such as apple, is best

Sheets of paper
You need some large pieces of paper to line the floor of the hutch. Old drawing paper or newspaper is ideal.

Shredded paper
Buy shredded paper bedding. Your guinea pigs will make their beds in the soft paper.

Hay
Get some dry, fresh hay. Guinea pigs love to eat hay and will also use it to make their beds.

Gnawing log
Find a small tree branch for your guinea pigs to gnaw on. Gnawing helps to keep their teeth healthy.

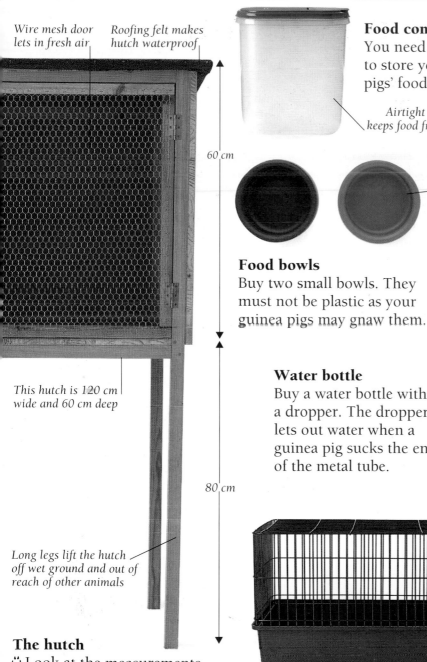

Wire mesh door lets in fresh air

Roofing felt makes hutch waterproof

60 cm

This hutch is 120 cm wide and 60 cm deep

Long legs lift the hutch off wet ground and out of reach of other animals

80 cm

The hutch
❀ Look at the measurements in the picture. Your pets' hutch should be at least this big. The hutch should have two rooms. The large room is used for eating. The smaller room is used as a bedroom. Your guinea pigs will make their beds and hide in it.

Food container
You need a container to store your guinea pigs' food.

Airtight box keeps food fresh

Heavy bowl is hard to tip over

Food bowls
Buy two small bowls. They must not be plastic as your guinea pigs may gnaw them.

Water bottle
Buy a water bottle with a dropper. The dropper lets out water when a guinea pig sucks the end of the metal tube.

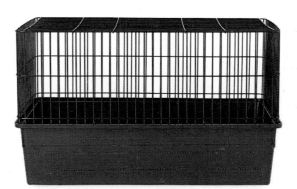

A home for indoor guinea pigs
You can keep your pigs indoors. They need a small cage to sleep in. Make them a fun box to play and eat in when they are awake.

Where to put the hutch

Make sure cats and wild animals can't get into the hutch

Your guinea pigs will get too hot in bright sunshine

Shelter the hutch from wind and rain

Your guinea pigs will freeze if left out in the bitter cold

Put the hutch in a place where you can look at it often

Things to get ready

You will need to get some special things to help you look after your new pets. Do not put anything made of plastic in their hutch or fun box, as your guinea pigs will chew everything. Make sure you have got all the things ready before you fetch your guinea pigs.

Air hole

Carrying box
Ask your vet for a pet carrying box in which to carry your guinea pigs. It should have holes to let in air so your guinea pigs can breathe.

Towel   Water jug   Shampoo

Hot water bottle   Washing-up bowl

Squeaky clean
Sometimes you will need to wash your guinea pigs. Buy special shampoo. Find an old washing-up bowl to use as a bath and a jug to pour water. You will need a towel to dry your pets, and a hot water bottle to keep them warm as they dry.

Brush has soft bristles

Comb with rounded prongs

Brush and comb
Your guinea pigs' hair may become tangled. Buy a small, soft brush and fine comb to help you untangle it.

Brush   Comb

Weighing tray

Weighing scales
You will need to weigh your guinea pigs on kitchen scales to check that they are healthy. Line the tray with paper if you can't find old scales.

Cleaning equipment

To clean your guinea pigs' hutch, you will need special things. Never take things that are used to clean your house. Ask your vet which type of disinfectant spray to buy. Keep the cleaning equipment together, so that it is not used to clean anything else.

The fun box

You can make an indoor fun box for your guinea pigs and fill it with things for them to play with. Playing in the fun box will keep your pets fit and happy if you can't let them outside.

Washing-up liquid   Disinfectant spray   Bucket

Rubber gloves   Brush   Dustpan

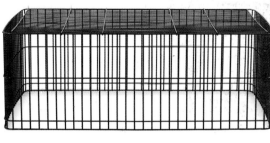

Indoor cage lid

If you keep your guinea pigs indoors, you should sometimes let them outside so they can eat grass. Put the top of their cage over them so they can't run away.

Scrubbing brush   Scraper   Bottle brush   Spout brush   Cleaning cloth

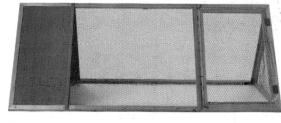

Grazing ark

Make or buy a grazing ark so that your guinea pigs can run around and graze outside. The ark must have a shaded area so they can shelter from the sun or hide if they are scared.

Choosing your guinea pigs

 You should get at least two guinea pigs. A guinea pig will be lonely living by itself. The guinea pigs must be the same sex. Get adults that live together already, or choose babies from a litter when they are at least six weeks old. If you want to keep lots of pigs, choose females. More than two males together will fight.

Where to find your new guinea pigs
- A friend's guinea pig may have babies.
- A breeder will sell you a breed of pig.
- An animal shelter may have guinea pigs of all kinds that need new homes.

Five-week pup

Beautiful adult

Babies or adults?
It is easy to fall in love with tiny baby guinea pigs. These are called puppies. But remember, they will soon grow up. Adult guinea pigs can be just as adorable.

Short hair is easy to look after

Long hair must be brushed regularly

Long hair or short hair?
Long-haired guinea pigs look lovely but their coats need lots of special care. The coats of short-haired guinea pigs don't get so untidy.

Look for lively guinea pigs that like to play

Owner points at the babies

Shy baby pig hides

Bold baby explores the coconut shell

Mother nibbles on cucumber

1 **When you go to choose** a baby guinea pig, don't touch any of the puppies at first. Watch with the owner from a place where you won't disturb the puppies.

2 Ask the owner to pick up the baby that seems liveliest. Ask whether it is a male or a female. Check that the guinea pig hasn't been chosen by someone else.

Look to see if the baby is friendly

Stroke the baby gently

This curious young guinea pig looks out

Timid baby snuggles up to its mother

Shoe box makes a good hiding place

3 The owner will let you hold the puppy. Make sure you are sitting down. Hold the baby close to your chest so it feels safe. Now decide if you really like it.

Put one hand over the back

Put your other hand underneath the baby's bottom

Look to see if the guinea pig has clear eyes

Feel the fur – it should be soft

4 Check that the guinea pig is healthy. It should have a plump, well-fed body. It should have bright eyes and a clean nose and ears. Its fur should be shiny and silky all over, including under its bottom.

Welcome home

Your guinea pig may be frightened when it first leaves its mother. If you get two babies, they will keep each other company. If you already have a guinea pig and are introducing a new friend, watch carefully when they first meet. Have the hutch ready to help all your pets settle down together.

Vet listens to pig's heartbeat through his stethoscope

Visiting your vet

You should arrange to visit your vet on the way home from collecting your new guinea pig. The vet will examine it all over to make sure it is healthy. Your vet will be able to answer any questions that you have about your new pet.

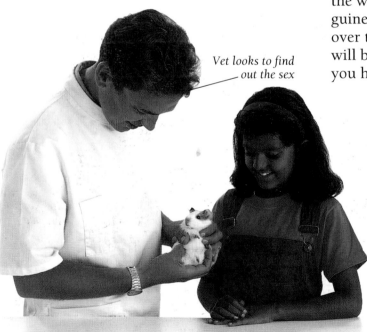

Vet looks to find out the sex

Male guinea pig

Female guinea pig

Checking the sex

When a guinea pig is very young, it can be hard to tell whether it is a male or a female. Ask your vet to check the sex of your guinea pig, so you are sure it is the sex you wanted.

Male and female

These pictures will help you find out the sex of your guinea pig. Look underneath, between its back legs.

Handling your pet
This chart tells you when to handle your new pets during the first two weeks.

When to handle your new guinea pigs

Day 1: Watch your pets, but don't disturb them.

Day 2: Your guinea pigs may hide in their beds. Talk to them, so they get used to your voice.

Day 3: Offer your pets food from your hand. Pick them up. Hold on firmly if they wriggle.

Days 4 – 7: Stroke and brush your pets. Show them to your family, and to other pets.

Days 8 – 11: Let your guinea pigs explore their outdoor enclosure, grazing ark and fun box.

After 2 weeks: Play with your pets every day.

Your guinea pig's home
Everything your pet needs should be in the hutch – bedding, food, water and a gnawing log. Put your new guinea pig into the hutch and leave it to explore its new home.

Fill the bedroom with shredded paper and hay

Line the floor with a layer of paper

...d hay for ...ood and for bedding

...wl should ...lled with fresh food

Bolt the door after you put the pig in the hutch

Attach the bottle, filled with fresh water, to the door

Open the door wide, so you can reach every area

Friends for your pets

Just like you, your guinea pigs like to have a lot of friends. Don't worry if they scuttle off to hide when you try to pick them up. Your guinea pigs are not being unfriendly – just shy. Another guinea pig makes the best friend for your guinea pig. But you, your family and some other pets all make good guinea pig friends.

Guinea pig feels safe close to its friends

In good company

You can keep lots of female guinea pigs together. Guinea pigs hate to be on their own. They never stray far from each other when they are eating. When they sleep, they huddle together. This keeps them warm.

Introducing a newcomer

When you choose a new friend for your guinea pigs, be careful. Remember that females in a group, or a male on its own, will fight a new adult. It is always best to introduce a new guinea pig that is about six weeks old.

Adult pig sniffs new baby pig

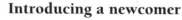

Baby pig looks timid

Keeping male guinea pigs

You must not keep more than two male guinea pigs together in a hutch. A group of males will fight. Choose two baby males from the same litter. If you already have a male, get a male friend that is about six weeks old.

This male guinea pig gets on well with its brother

Watch the animals all the time

Meeting the family dog

👫 Always ask an adult if you can let your guinea pig meet a dog. A quiet dog will not usually harm your guinea pig, but keep a firm grip on the dog's collar. Never leave them alone together.

Make sure the dog lies down

Be ready to pick your guinea pig up

Friend or foe?

A rabbit can sometimes be friends with a guinea pig. But they may also argue. When a rabbit gets cross with a guinea pig, it may kick it. A rabbit's back legs are very strong and the kick will hurt badly. Never keep a rabbit and a guinea pig in the same hutch.

Powerful back legs can kick out

Sharp claws

Part of the family

Show your family and friends how to hold your guinea pigs properly (see p21). They feel happiest being stroked on a lap. Don't leave your pets alone with a younger brother or sister.

Let your baby brother stroke your pet while you hold it

Always sit down to hold a guinea pig

Guinea pig feels safe cradled on a lap

Feeding your guinea pigs

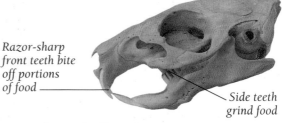

Guinea pigs are herbivores, which means that they only eat grass and plants. In the wild, they eat seeds and wild grasses. To keep your pets fit, you must feed them the same kinds of things. You should give them specially prepared guinea pig food and fresh food (see p28). Feed only small amounts of any new type of food.

Razor-sharp front teeth bite off portions of food

Side teeth grind food

Mouth made for chewing
The food your guinea pigs eat needs to be very well chewed. A guinea pig's teeth and mouth are specially made for biting and grinding. The food is mixed with spit in the mouth while it is ground by the teeth.

Dry mix

Dry fibre food

Grazing all day
Grass and some wild plants are favourite foods for guinea pigs. They have to eat a lot of greens to get enough goodness. Given the chance, your guinea pig will spend most of the day nibbling.

Special foods
Even if your guinea pigs graze on grass, you need to give them other food. They love hay, which is dried grass. You must also buy them special foods made from mixtures of dried plants, seeds and vegetables.

Hay

A guinea pig spends a lot of time eating

When to feed your guinea pigs
Feed your pets every morning and evening. Guinea pigs must always have dry food to eat. They don't make a store of food, like squirrels or hamsters.

✷ Eating droppings

Don't worry if you see your guinea pigs eating their own droppings – all guinea pigs do this. Their stomachs can't take out all the goodness from the food the first time they eat it. So they make soft droppings, which they eat again.

Fresh water

Wild guinea pigs get water from the fresh food they eat. Your guinea pigs eat a lot of dry food, so you must make sure their water bottle is always full.

Fasten the bottle where the guinea pigs can easily reach it

Tip of tube has a little ball to stop water dripping when no-one is drinking

Tongue licks the tube tip to make the water flow

Screw lid on tightly

Pour new food into bowl morning and evening

Cheeks suck in when gnawing

Apple tree log is best

Grinding down the teeth

Your guinea pigs' teeth grow all the time. Wild guinea pigs gnaw trees. This helps to keep their teeth short. Give your pets a log to gnaw. This will stop their teeth from growing too long.

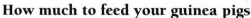

How much to feed your guinea pigs

Each time you feed your guinea pigs, fill the bowls to the brim. Your pets should only eat as much food as they need. If they have plenty of exercise, they won't get fat.

Feeding fresh foods

 Eating salads and fresh fruit every day helps to keep you healthy. These foods are full of goodness. Just like you, your guinea pigs need to eat fresh foods. Give them spare fruit and vegetables from the kitchen, and collect wild plants. But be careful! Some wild plants are poisonous. Look on this page to see the wild plants that are safe for your pets to eat.

Grass

Shepherd's purse

Clover

Wild plant food
👬 Twice a week, gather a few handfuls of grass and safe weeds to feed your guinea pigs. You can also let them graze on fresh grass and plants (see p39).

Dandelion

Good food game
Try hiding your guinea pigs' food in a brick, or under a heap of hay. Fresh food smells very strongly. Your guinea pigs will have fun sniffing it out.

Plantain

Clever guinea pig has found the food

This guinea pig smells the food but can't see it

🐾 Food must be fresh
Fresh plants, fruit and vegetables quickly become stale. Throw away these foods if they haven't been eaten by bedtime. Never give your guinea pigs grass cuttings as they go mouldy very quickly.

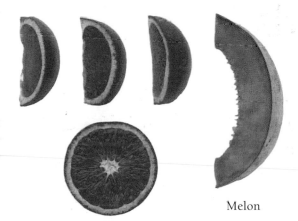

Pear

Apple

Grapes

Tomato

Favourite fruit

👥 Feed one slice of fresh fruit to each of your guinea pigs every day. Apple and pear slices may be chopped into small pieces to make them easier to nibble.

Orange

Melon

Crunchy vegetables

👥 Every day, chop up a handful of vegetables to give to each of your guinea pigs. Your greengrocer may be able to give you scraps that are suitable. Make sure they are fresh.

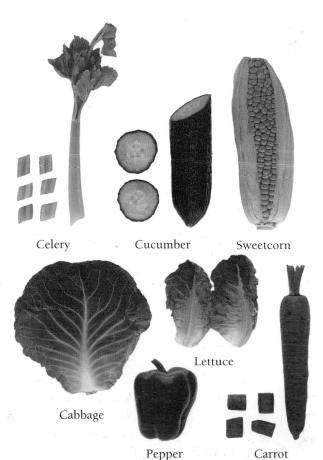

Celery

Cucumber

Sweetcorn

Cabbage

Lettuce

Pepper

Carrot

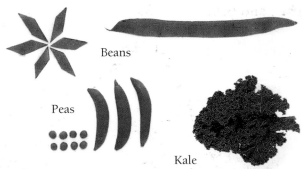

Beans

Peas

Kale

Vital vitamin

Just like you, guinea pigs need vitamin C to keep them healthy. Make sure you feed your guinea pigs a food that is rich in vitamin C every day. Give each one a quarter of an orange or a large handful of fresh cabbage or kale.

Cleaning the hutch

Your guinea pigs like their home to be very clean. If their hutch becomes dirty, it will start to smell. Your guinea pigs will become ill. You should clean out the hutch and wash the feeding equipment every day. Put new paper and fresh bedding, hay, food and water in the hutch when you have finished. Once a week, scrub the hutch out thoroughly.

Don't forget to take out the bowls

Put the guinea pig bottom first into the box

1 **Every day, put your pets** into their carrying box, one by one. This will keep them safely out of the way so you can clean their hutch. On a nice day, you could let them graze outside in their grazing ark (see p39).

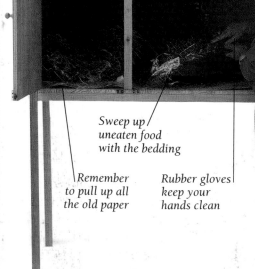

Sweep up uneaten food with the bedding

Remember to pull up all the old paper

Rubber gloves keep your hands clean

Door opens wide so you can reach to clean

2 **Use your dustpan and brush** to sweep up old bedding, droppings and stale food. Remember to wear your rubber gloves. Lift up all the lining paper. Throw everything away into a dustbin.

Do not scrape too hard, or you will damage the wood

Washing bowls

Wipe out each of the food bowls with the cleaning cloth. You might need to soak them if they are very dirty. Dry them with kitchen paper.

Wipe right into the corners

3 Use your scraper to lift off any bits stuck to the floor or sides of the hutch. The corners are often dirtiest. Sweep up with the dustpan and brush.

Clearing the dropper

Make sure nothing is blocking the bottle dropper. Brush the tube with the spout brush. Then shake the tube. You should hear the metal ball moving around.

Twist the brush inside the tube

Spray to kill germs

Bucket with hot water and a squirt of detergent

Turn the brush to clean the inside

Thorough clean

Once a week, use a brush and hot, soapy water to scrub the inside of the hutch. Rinse the hutch and then spray it with disinfectant. Leave it to dry out.

Cleaning the bottle

Pour hot, soapy water into the water bottle. Scrub the sides with the bottle brush. Rinse out the water bottle before filling it with fresh water.

Good grooming

 Brush your guinea pigs every day so that they get used to you stroking and handling them. Long-haired and rough-haired guinea pigs will get dirt and hay stuck in their coats. Grooming keeps the hair clean and tangle-free. Wash your pets if their coats become smelly and greasy.

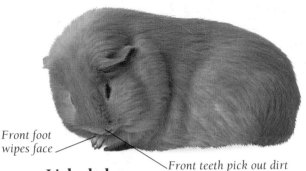

Front foot wipes face

Front teeth pick out dirt

Licked clean
A guinea pig spends a lot of time grooming itself. It uses its front teeth as a comb and its tongue as a flannel. It can also use its back claws as combs.

Brushing all over
To groom a long-haired guinea pig, brush the hair on its back away from its head. Then brush its tummy and under its chin.

Brush the hair in the direction it grows

Use one hand to keep your guinea pig still

Tell your guinea pig not to be afraid

Put one hand on its back

Place one hand underneath the pig to support it

Combing the coat
After brushing, change to using the comb. Comb the back, and then under the chin. Untangle knots with your fingers.

Pull the comb gently through the hair

1 **To wash a guinea pig**, first lower it carefully into a washing-up bowl filled with a little warm water. It may wriggle, so hold on firmly.

2 Splash water onto the coat, but keep the face dry. Pour a capful of the special shampoo onto the back. Rub it into the coat with the tips of your fingers.

Rub shampoo in underneath as well as on top

Guinea pig looks white and foamy

Shampoo is from the vet

3 Give your guinea pig a shower to rinse it. Pour warm water from the jug over its neck. Rub the water into its coat. Keep pouring and rubbing until there are no more bubbles in the coat.

Jug filled with warm water

Hold the head up high so the suds run off the back

4 Put your guinea pig onto the towel. Before it shakes itself and soaks you, quickly fold the towel around it. Rub your pet dry. When you unfold the towel, all its hair will be standing up. Brush and comb the hair gently.

Rub the coat all over with the towel

5 Put your guinea pig in the carrying box. Wrap the hot water bottle in a clean towel. Put the bottle in the box to keep the guinea pig warm. Place the box in a warm room. When the guinea pig is completely dry, put it back in the hutch.

Hot water bottle covered in a towel

Hay makes a cosy bed

Understanding guinea pigs

Guinea pigs show their mood by moving parts of their bodies. They mark the things that belong to them with their scent. They make lots of noises, from a purr to a squeal. Watch them, and you will soon understand what they are doing.

Nose sniffs the air

Eyes search

Neck is stretched

Sniffing

Smelly clues

Guinea pigs sniff the air to discover if there is anyone else close by. When two guinea pigs meet, they smell each other to find out whether or not they are friends. They may sniff each other's nose, or bottom.

Sniffing the bottom of a stranger to see if it's a friend

Sniffing bottoms

Marking what's mine

Just like you, your guinea pigs label the things they own. Instead of writing their names on them, they leave their scent. The scent is in the skin on their cheeks, backs and bottoms. It is also in the grease that comes from the grease gland at the base of the back.

Nose picks up other guinea pig's scent

Sniffing nose to nose

Dragging bottom

Scent is left as bottom slides along the ground

Rubbing cheeks

Scent is left on other guinea pig's cheek

Marking with grease

Grease is rubbed onto log

Still as a statue

Guinea pigs are very shy. When they hear a strange or loud sound, they do not move. Every hair on their body lies still. They think that if they freeze, an enemy won't spot them.

Fur is unruffled

Fur bristles up

Eyes stare at enemy

Angry guinea pig

Head twists away in fear

Timid guinea pig

Meeting the enemy

A guinea pig can get angry with another guinea pig. Its hair stands on end to make it look bigger. It makes a loud chattering sound to tell the other pig that it is annoyed.

The angry pig

When a guinea pig becomes furious, it yawns to show its razor-sharp teeth.

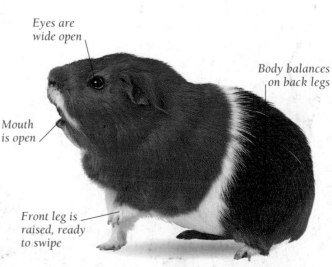

Mouth opens wide to show teeth

The boxing match

If both guinea pigs are brave, they will fight. They stand on their back legs and ram each other with their heads. They keep their mouths open, ready to bite.

Eyes are wide open

Body balances on back legs

Ears are perked up

Hair stands on end

Mouth is open

Front leg is raised, ready to swipe

The enclosure

Guinea pigs love to be outside. Ask an adult to fence off a grassy area of your garden to make an enclosure. Stand the hutch in a sheltered corner. Search around your house and garden for things to put in the area for your guinea pigs to play with. Make a ramp so your pets can climb down from the hutch into their playground.

Bottle filled with fresh water

Guinea pig hides in large pipe

Rocks to shelter behind

Clay pipe to run through

Small log to gnaw

Holes in brick make a perfect hiding place for food

A few stones make a good hide-out

Things to collect
Try and find bricks, stones and clay pipes to put in the enclosure. Guinea pigs love to explore new things.

Plastic sheet can be pulled over area when it rains

Wire mesh to protect area from other animals

Carrot to nibble

Rungs on the ramp stop guinea pigs from slipping

Prowling cats may jump into the area

Birds of prey may swoop down

Weedkillers on the grass are poisonous

Dogs may scare your guinea pigs

Some plants will poison guinea pigs

Protect the enclosure from bright sun and bad weather

The guinea pig enclosure
It is fun to watch your guinea pigs play in the enclosure. Try to understand what they are doing (see p34). If you're not inside the enclosure, cover it with mesh to stop other animals getting in. Protect the area with plastic if it rains.

Things to do with your pets

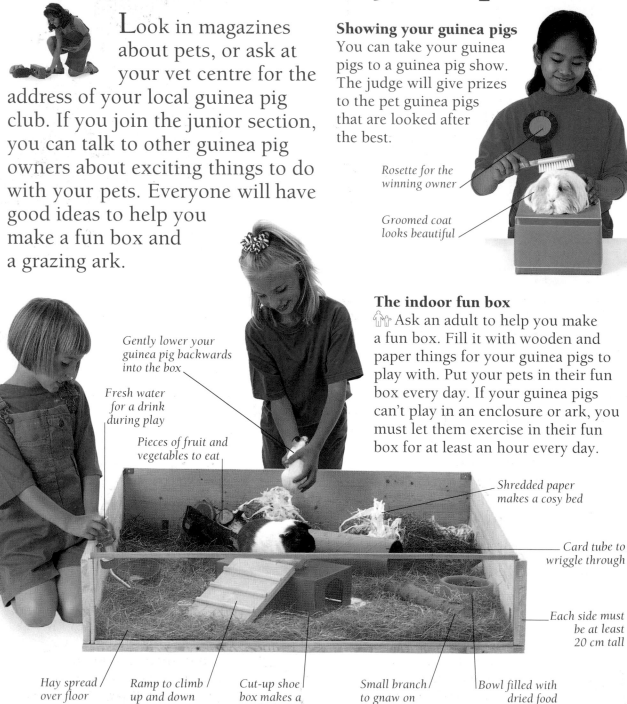

Look in magazines about pets, or ask at your vet centre for the address of your local guinea pig club. If you join the junior section, you can talk to other guinea pig owners about exciting things to do with your pets. Everyone will have good ideas to help you make a fun box and a grazing ark.

Showing your guinea pigs

You can take your guinea pigs to a guinea pig show. The judge will give prizes to the pet guinea pigs that are looked after the best.

Rosette for the winning owner

Groomed coat looks beautiful

The indoor fun box

Ask an adult to help you make a fun box. Fill it with wooden and paper things for your guinea pigs to play with. Put your pets in their fun box every day. If your guinea pigs can't play in an enclosure or ark, you must let them exercise in their fun box for at least an hour every day.

Gently lower your guinea pig backwards into the box

Fresh water for a drink during play

Pieces of fruit and vegetables to eat

Shredded paper makes a cosy bed

Card tube to wriggle through

Each side must be at least 20 cm tall

Hay spread over floor

Ramp to climb up and down

Cut-up shoe box makes a good playhouse

Small branch to gnaw on

Bowl filled with dried food

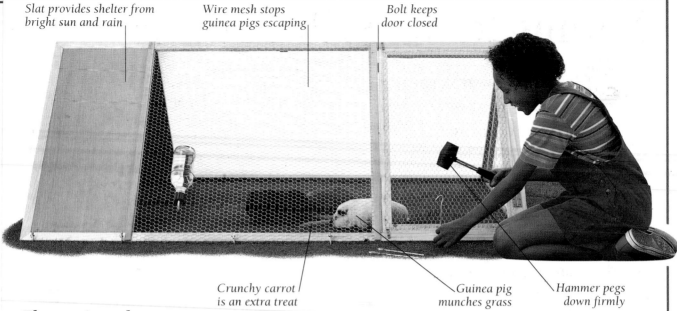

Slat provides shelter from bright sun and rain

Wire mesh stops guinea pigs escaping

Bolt keeps door closed

Crunchy carrot is an extra treat

Guinea pig munches grass

Hammer pegs down firmly

The grazing ark

In dry weather, you can put your guinea pigs out on grass in a grazing ark for an hour a day. Peg the ark down so that your guinea pigs can't tip it up, and other animals can't get inside. Move the ark every day, so your guinea pigs always have fresh grass to nibble.

Leaving your guinea pigs

Going on holiday
You can't always take your guinea pigs with you when you go on holiday. You must find someone to look after them. You may have a friend with guinea pigs who has time to look after yours as well.

Making a check list
Make a list of the jobs that need doing every day. Write them down in the order that you do them. Your guinea pigs are used to this order and may be upset if your friend changes it. Also make a note of the name and telephone number of your vet.

What to pack
Get everything ready for your friend. Make sure you pack enough food. Don't forget all the cleaning and grooming equipment.

Moving your guinea pigs
Take your guinea pigs to your friend in their carrying box or small cage. Bring their fun box or grazing ark if your friend has nowhere for your pets to exercise.